12 Ways to Hug Yourself

Bonnie Block

PublishAmerica
Baltimore

First printing

ISBN: 1-4137-7419-9
PUBLISHED BY PUBLISHAMERICA, LLLP
www.publishamerica.com
Baltimore

Printed in the United States of America

I dedicate this book to my husband, Alan, and my children, Barbie, Julie and Mike. I am so very grateful to have them in my life. I hope that they will always believe in the beauty of their dreams.

"The future belongs to those who believe in the beauty of their dreams."
Eleanor Roosevelt

Acknowledgments

Special thanks to Micki Mez
for capturing the essence of who I am
in all of the illustrations.

Table of Contents

October 2, 2001

Dear Friends,

I had the wonderful opportunity of attending two Facilitating Skills Seminars by Jack Canfield, co-author of the Chicken Soup for the Soul series. In one of the workshops, he shared the importance of reciting daily affirmations as well as the various steps for their creation. As a result of those presentations, just about every morning, I have read my note cards denoting things I'm affirming to happen in my life.

Concluding this book has been a goal written and rewritten on many a note card. It seems as if I have had these great intentions of finishing this manuscript by a certain date and then appear on Oprah's show to share the message. And then...I stopped writing. I did not stop thinking about it...I just stopped writing.

September 11, 2001—the horrific disaster that changed life for everyone. My son worked in New York. He witnessed the attacks from the window of his office two and a half miles away. Physically he was spared, as were each of us that viewed it from afar. However, I believe that each of us will be emotionally scarred forever.

During that tragic time, I remember being told over and over again by our country's leaders that we must, "go back to our normal schedules." I thought how could our lives ever be normal again?

As parents I believe that we model for our children every day of our lives, no matter what the circumstances. After September 11, my grief as well as the pain my children felt from this disaster laid heavy on my heart. Immediately, I began focusing on how I could make their hurt go away, just as I tried to do when they were little. My first innocent thought was that perhaps we could just talk it away. Realistically I knew the answer would be much more complex.

I continued to watch the daily news and read into the wee hours of the morning as if to find some magical cure to make the world not such a scary place to live. At times, I remembered feeling so inadequate as to how I could possibly help my children, the victims and their families as well as my country. I really wanted to find a way that could in some

9

small part help our world. It was then that I began to think about my unfinished book. The message, I believed, would correspond to one's feelings when snuggling under a cozy blanket on a stormy night. The surge to write began again.

Today as I was writing at home, I reread the affirmation over my desk that related to my completing this task. It states, "I am gratefully rejoicing that God and I are creating *12 Ways to Hug Yourself* together and it is fabulous." I do believe that God helps one do everything in life. He is with us always. Perhaps, this is why I did not conclude the book in the past. Now was the time it was needed more than ever.

After September 11, 2001, I felt the world became like one big family. This book is also dedicated to each of you. May you receive God's blessings every day. I hope that you will always believe in your dreams.

BB

Preface

It is December 30, 1999, my fifty-seventh birthday. In one more day, it will be a new millennium, the year 2000. It is hard for me to imagine that I have already lived that many years. It is also just as hard for me to imagine that I am going to write this book. I look for miracles every day in my life, as you will read in a future chapter. I believe this book is one of my miracles. This is how it all began....

I had been in environments where authors were abundant. I had often looked at them with awe. When I was present in such company, I would ponder the idea of writing a book, never passionately feeling that I was truly qualified to convey a message nor had a topic to share that others would benefit from reading. However, to my amazement, I began to obtain this very strong desire and commitment to begin such a project. I found myself sharing my aspiration with others and visualizing fulfilling this dream. Would you believe it all began with a workshop?

Over the years, I have devoted myself to helping others become esteemed. I have recognized the great need for caregivers to feel lovable, capable and special. I understood what a nurturing environment appreciated individuals were capable of creating. I knew from firsthand experiences how contagious these elements were for empowerment and so I created the workshop "12 Ways to Hug Yourself."

In my profession, I have created and presented various quality trainings, especially on enhancing one's self-esteem. For several years, I presented this highly acclaimed workshop for various groups. The appeal of the presentation grew in abundance and never ceased to put me in a state of awe. The sessions appeared to have broken down some internal barriers. It allowed participants to feel safe to embrace and be embraced, which is a basic need in all of us.

This feeling was exhibited in various behaviors at the conclusions of the workshop: participants immediately reached out to me with a hug; participants requested additional materials to take home to review; participants expressed a strong desire to recapture and retain the feelings of self-worth gained during the workshop; participants shared the desire to carry the messages to their families and friends; and the participants wrote and phoned beautiful messages. Believing that each of us has a responsibility to help create a kinder world and seeing the transformation of those I had been able to touch through those presentations, I decided to pursue becoming a published author.

And I just began writing! I remember looking at the first completed thoughts that were on paper and feeling disbelief of my actions. Was I really going to write this book? I had never attempted anything like this before. When I had stretched myself into unknown territories, it was always to benefit others. This project did indeed have the same ultimate goal.

Looking for help, I wrote on the bottom of the paper, "Lord, show me the way. Guide me in the writing of this book." To my amazement, the first words of a chapter were written. Then at the conclusion of the draft of the first chapter, I questioned what was I going to compose next. Before I realized it, that day, or a few days later, at anytime day or night, the topic of the next chapter would come to mind.

I had stopped writing for a while and questioned my ability with my self-doubting mantra that many often play. I'd think, *Am I capable enough to write this? Will it be significant enough to have meaning for others?* Then another miracle happened!

I was on my way home from visiting my son in New York. I was traveling alone by bus. As I enjoy talking to people, I began to strike a conversation with a very nice woman sitting across from me. We talked about life, gave opinions, and solved many societal issues. She told me she was a writer. I began to share my dream again and asked her for advice for a budding new author. "Just keep writing. Just keep doing it!" she remarked. "Don't look back, just spring forward."

Her words became an infusion of energetic spirit! Enthusiastically, I went back to my writing. Each time I ceased writing for a while or had seemed to lose my way in this task, I kept hearing my mentor's words, "Just keep writing. Just keep doing it!"

I feel that the key to the success of the messages in *12 Ways To Hug Yourself* is to be open to practicing the strategies without focusing on being perfect. Toddlers learn to walk through taking risks; crawling, standing, holding on to a secure object, and then taking that memorable first step alone. They continue to move forward in the accomplishing of their task of leaning to walk, meeting all the challenges head on or, really, bottoms up!

I believe toddlers can achieve many goals because someone is always there cheerleading for them, always recognizing their efforts. Let us learn from this familiar scenario and practice being first our own internal cheerleader as we set forth to reach our many goals. Then we will be able to assume that role for others in a much more capable and meaningful fashion.

My suggestions for reading this book would be:

- Take your time and enjoy the book for the first time for pure enjoyment.
- Reread the book a second time and reflect on various aspects that pertain to your quality of life. Please be mindful that the strategies are not sequential.
- Practice the hugs you feel comfortable with, perhaps with a buddy. Try some that may not be your first choice. (Remember, past research has claimed that it takes 21 days to make a habit.)
- Review a chapter(s) after several weeks of originally completing the text. I continue to reread some of my favorite books as the words create new meaning for me as I encounter additional life experiences.

Friends, I truly believe this book has been spiritually inspired and that it is a special gift to ourselves, one to pick up when our emotional bank account is on low or when we have given all we have to others and have left nothing for our own needs.

I hope my message will inspire and motivate you to hug yourself often throughout the day and to open your arms and hearts to hug others.

Do You Like Getting Gifts?

I can't see or hear your reaction, but if you are just a little bit like me I bet you love them! There are many types of gifts one can get: candy, flowers, trips, jewelry, etc. They can come in all sizes and shapes. Again, if you are like me, any gift given in a loving, inviting manner would be highly appreciated!

Have you ever given or received an unusual present? One of the most unusual presents I received was a package filled with chocolate-covered candy cars. This package came right after I had the unfortunate experience of having my car stolen. My good friend went out of her way to send me a surprise hug in the mail and I gratefully received it.

The most unusual gift I ever gave was a Celebration of Life party. One of my best friends had been a cancer survivor for five years. I wanted to find a means to mark this wonderful occasion. I decided to plan an evening for her friends and family to openly share how much she meant to everyone. My friend had the opportunity to express joy and gratitude for their friendship and loving support during this difficult life passage. Each one of us left that evening receiving so many lessons about life. It was, indeed, a very treasured moment.

I wanted to give you a very special gift. I knew just what to give you. I did not need your favorite color or your size. With your busy lifestyle, I knew you would not like to spend time assembling the surprise. There will not be any artificial ingredients contained in the present nor will it pollute the environment. Research has even stated that it can protect you against illness, reduce depression, strengthen family relationships, help you to sleep better, and be easy to exchange. I just knew that even if you had one, you would surely want another.

What was this outstanding, remarkable gift that I really wanted to present you with? It was a HUG!!!

I want to share 12 ways to hug yourself. In my self-help education, I've learned that each one of us needs 12 hugs daily in order to blossom and continue our personal growth.

The ideal scenario would be if each of us would receive at least 12 hugs (and perhaps even more) on a daily basis from individuals that we meet during the day. When I taught kindergarten to thirty-two wonderful five-year-olds, my days were filled with hugs. With the way of our society—computers, answering machines, fax machines, e-mail—one cannot even get to have a conversation with a person, let alone receive a personal hug!

With the following strategies, you will be able to blossom by assuming responsibilities for your own 12 hugs. When you receive the additional hugs, it will be like having hot fudge sauce placed on an already delicious ice cream sundae!

Eat Something Forbidden

"The quality of your choices affects the quality of your life."
Bonnie Block

Have you ever been on vacation and unconsciously seemed to have given yourself permission to eat anything you wanted? My husband and I took our family on a cruise to celebrate our 35th wedding anniversary. All of us are usually very health conscious, especially when it comes to our diets. Before the cruise, each of us found ourselves trying to get our bodies in extra great shape knowing that we would probably be exposed to some awesome food. Right before our journey began, we agreed to spend every waking moment on the much-awaited trip in enjoyment, including giving ourselves permission to indulge in the goodies of our choice. We also promised not to check what each other had chosen to eat.

Cruise time came to be pig out time. I seemed to do okay during the morning and early afternoon hours, but from then on, the food intake valve in my body was on overactive. I even found myself waiting for the late night buffet to open to have a hotdog. When I am on my own turf at home, I have a very limited intake of that particular food due to my cholesterol. On board the ship, I began making this item a regular part of my nightly entertainment. My perfect rationale was that they were the most delicious hot dogs I had ever eaten!

Reflecting on my vacations at the beach in the summer, it seems that I followed the same mode of behavior. Boardwalk fries at any time, sticky apples, hot doughnuts, molasses lollipops, the list could go on. All seem to be part of the sunshine and my relaxation. This habit made me feel good at the time and place it occurred, especially when I was not having a great moment. Silently, I would began to sing the mantra, "It's okay. I deserve to have that!"

I once heard a beautifully shaped movie star comment on how she maintained her terrific figure. She didn't deny herself anything but limited the amount she consumed of her favorite product. The woman shared that she took a bite or two of everything she wanted and then removed it from in front of her. (What self discipline! Ugh! And what a figure! Amazing!) She took care of her desires and did not seem to carry the burden of having to please others. Bill Cosby seemed to sum up that philosophy when he stated, "I do not know the key to success, but the key to failure is trying to please everybody!"

I knew friends that kept chocolate in their purses and when they felt they needed a hug, they placed a piece of that sweet morsel in their mouths. Whatever helps you receive your first hug, give yourself permission and go for it (if only in moderation).

I am reflecting back on another special time in my life when I gave myself permission to eat anything I wanted. It was after my yearly gynecological visit. I dreaded that exam and big weigh-in. Afterwards, I made certain that I rewarded myself with a delicious treat filled with many calories, regardless of what number was on the doctor's scale (perhaps the scale was wrong due to the humidity in the air). Any excuse would do in order for me to have this hug! I could hear the candies calling me. "Bonnie, come get a hug for yourself." And I listened!

This first hug is easy to do; however, the special, acquired feeling does not last long even though the weight from the calories can last a lifetime.

The remaining hugs are, by far, much more difficult to become disciplined at accomplishing but they are guaranteed to last much longer. That will be the grand prize for all of our efforts.

Let's go for it. Together we can do it! Let's model our thoughts after the little engine in the children's book, *The Little Engine That Could.* The little engine began her journey to take the toys to the children by saying, "I cannot, I cannot." Eventually, the engine began saying, "I think I can, I think I can," and achieved the goal. At the end, we read that the little blue engine says, "I thought I could, I thought I could!"

Please join me as we begin.

"Time is not an obstacle to one who chooses to succeed."
Alan Cohen

Give Yourself Positive Messages

"If you believe it, you can achieve it."
Robert H. Schuller

Do you talk to yourself? When someone asked me this question I found my first reaction to be, me? Talk to myself? Why I guess I do. Then I began to smile and laugh as I began to realize what I had just done.

I really believe that this hug—"give yourself positive messages"—is one of the hardest hugs we need to follow for a healthy, happy life. The good news is that with regular practice, it is an eternal gift that we can give ourselves that will provide us with many quality moments.

One day I was feeling sad and frustrated. I was thinking about various things that I wish I knew how to do and do well (play the guitar, paint with watercolor and oils, sing, and play every instrument in the orchestra, just to mention a few). I remember sending those messages to myself on a regular basis throughout the day. Really, if I were to be very honest, I think I had sent many negative messages on other days too.

At times, I would hear myself stating to others that I was a Jack of All Trades and Master of None. What did I really excel at? Was I really great at anything? On the days where I expressed negative sentiments, everything I seemed to do or touch did not meet my expectations or goals. I am not certain what brought this reaction on but it was destroying the quality of my life.

One of my children happened to call the house when I was in the midst of one of these emotional times. I shared openly about my feelings. My child responded by stating how lucky I was because I had always been interested in many areas not just one. The acknowledgment by my child that I was enough was wonderful and I became comforted by those thoughts. However, there was still a small voice of negativity that was lingering.

Later that evening, I quietly sat in my bed reflecting on all the things I could do. The list went on and on. I could feel my level of self-esteem rising as I was recalling in detail many of my various accomplishments and talents. I then reviewed which ones I would have wanted to give up in order to have had the time and perhaps the money to reach other unaccomplished goals. The answer was none.

Then the positive messages began to pour into my brain. How lucky I was to have had and continue to have so many interests, talents, and experiences. By the time this positive, internal dialogue was completed, I felt great. The little aches of negativism throughout my body went away, and I had recaptured the feeling of IALACS—"I am lovable and capable and special," a term used to denote positive self-esteem by Jack Canfield.

It has been stated that individuals talk to themselves all day long. Some say we internalize 90,000 thoughts a day, and about 5,000 thoughts an hour. Most of those thoughts have been categorized as negative. While I have shared one of my internal, negative tales, I feel certain that each if us can recall many such experiences.

It has been noted that the brain can only contain one thought at a time. In our busy world, we often put this concept to test. Try holding one thought and writing down another one. It is difficult to do. When we send any message to ourselves, our self-concept and our ability to perform are affected. Our negative talk, sometimes referred to as "stinkin' thinkin'," can often create a change in our bodies that is often less than desirable.

Our brain doesn't know if what we chose to place inside by our internal dialogue was real or something we perceived. Therefore, when we state internally, "I am a bad person," and we replay those negative tapes over and over again, the brain responds accordingly. When our choice is to state, "I am a good person," the brain will respond appropriately for that message. Our bodies come alive when we think positive thoughts. Our abilities expand; we become like butterflies that have just opened from the cocoon. The secret is we must choose to focus on the positive.

One of my favorite sayings is, "The quality of your choices equals the quality of your life." I believe when we chose to focus on the affirmative, hope stays alive, and we can climb up from any valley. It is our choice and our choice alone. We can work at staying healthy by exercising with all the right equipment and eating all the right foods. The question becomes how are we keeping our minds healthy? Being healthy reflects the total person, one's mind, body, and spirit. They are a terrific team and neither can be overlooked for achieving true total wellness. Healthy messages can often be the key spark that promotes our becoming and achieving good health.

Once again, the choice is ours. Is it difficult to accomplish? You bet! Sometimes I feel that it is an internal battle. There are even times when one feels that the war is over and then before we know it, a new one begins. A quote I am reminded of when such feelings begin to seep into my body is, "According to the effort is the reward" (author unknown). The choice is ours but so is the reward!

In the best-selling book, *Tuesdays with Morrie*, Ted Koppel interviewed Morrie Schwartz, a man who was living and dying with ALS. In the second interview, Mr. Koppel asked, "How will you give when you can no longer speak?'" Morrie responded, "Maybe I'll have everyone ask me yes and no questions."

Then Mr. Koppel inquired about Morrie's relationship with his good friend Maurie Stein. Maurie had a disease that was causing him to lose his sight. The anchorman was picturing the two buddies together one day where one would not be able to hear and the other would not be able to speak. He asked Morrie what he thought that experience would be like.

Responding in the positive, Morrie stated, "We will hold hands. And there'll be a lot of love passing between us." Morrie chose to find a positive anchor during those difficult times.

With all the pressures we feel from life, there are many reasons, whether consciously or unconsciously, to tend to give ourselves negative messages. I want to share some positive anchors for us to hold on to so we can remain above board while our ship is rocking.

Strategy 1

Recall a time in your life that was the ultimate, positive experience for you. Everything about it made you feel special. Concentrate on that experience, reflecting on the details. Write a brief description of the event. You may choose to note several words that will bring the memory back in full. Keep those thoughts in your wallet, around your home, and/or office. When an unpleasant situation occurs and you begin to put yourself down with negative thoughts, review your notes. Remember that the brain is capable of only holding one thought at a time. This technique will bring you back to a positive self-focus—a B12 type energizing shot for self-empowerment!

Strategy 2

Wear a colored rubber band around your wrist. Each time you find yourself recalling a negative situation that you are fearful of, angry about, etc., pull at the rubber band. This little shock will remind you to change your self-talk. This technique is especially great for a message that you seem to have engraved on your brain and is repeated over and over again throughout each hour of the day.

After a day or so, just look at the rubber band to obtain the same positive message. When I feel comfortable to go on to the next step, I place my rubber band somewhere in the car where I can see it. It seems I still desire some anchor for my message even though I may be over the intensity of the emotion. When I remove the rubber band entirely from my sight, I smile and feel so proud of the accomplishment. My self-esteem is very high on that day!

Strategy 3

When a negative situation comes along, reframe the problem. My girlfriend had radiation for cancer. She was scared of the disease as well as the cure. Rather than focus on the negative tales she had heard, she, like Morrie, chose to find a positive image. She began a daily self-talk of thanks; thanks for living at a time when a cure was possible, thanks for the scientist who invented the cure, and thanks for engineers who built the machines to utilize during the procedure. With her attitude of thanks maintained throughout her treatment, her recovery was most successful.

Strategy 4

Dr. Bernie Siegel notes the benefits of having rational concern in regards to problems. So often when a situation occurs that is negative, we begin to internalize, "What did I do? It was my fault! How can I fix it immediately? Life is over! I am a bad parent, child, friend, and/or person!"

Many times we know it just happened, but we seem to be so eager to take responsibility. This is especially true in many situations where children are involved. (Someone said if one is so eager to accept the blame for the bad then they must also be eager to be the cause for the good.) As we continue to feed the issue with so many negative sparks, the problem escalates into a glacier. Accept what happened, feel the emotion, and share it with several others. Shortly thereafter, review the details, brainstorm ways to move on with life and take action.

My pappy seemed to give up on life when his only son, my father, died at the age of 29. His life consisted of going to work and/or watching television. Life for my granny was never the same after this tragic event. However, my granny chose to remember him always with lots of love, and at the same time to live.

In one chapter in *Tuesdays with Morrie* (I guess you know by now I loved that book), Morrie shared his feelings about his disease during his interview with Ted Koppel. He detailed how he decided that he was going to live by saying, "I am going to live—or at least try to live—the way that I want, with dignity, with courage, with humor, with composure." He continued, "There are some mornings when I cry and cy and mourn for myself. Some mornings I'm so angry and bitter. But it doesn't last too long. Then I get up and say, I want to live." He then continued on in the day with his goal to live. I am so grateful that Mitch Albom shared his great teacher's lessons with the world.

When some centenarians, people who live to be 100, were asked for a secret to their long and quality life, they responded by stating they felt the pain of difficult times and then moved on. Ninety-two-year-old Papa Sam, a special person in our family, had a wife, a daughter, a daughter-in-law, and many relatives pass away. He was overcome with grief in all these deaths. His positive outlook for living enabled him to overcome these difficult times, not to forget, and to go forward with positive memories. That is the gift of this strategy.

Strategy 5

Create affirmations and state them daily. One of my morning affirmations is, "I am gratefully rejoicing that I am enough to reach all of my goals successfully and do not let my power or belief in myself be diminished by what others may say or do." This statement is so empowering to me as I read these words before beginning my day (sometimes, I will read them during the day and at night). A sense of peace comes over me each time I read them. I have a chance to focus just on myself and how I want to be. I am truly empowered by the statement.

Let me share how to create your own affirmations as taught to me in a self-esteem seminar. An affirmation is a short, direct, positive statement written as if you already have what you want or what you want has already been accomplished. Begin with "I am." Include an action word ending in "ing." Also include a dynamic feeling word in the statement.

Here is an example. You have a big event coming up in your life. You might state, "I am gratefully rejoicing that my (the event) is so very successful in every way." That keeps the positive focus present in your life. Whenever a negative message seeps into your mind, these affirmations quickly pop up to give your brain a positive jolt (please keep in mind that the affirmation is just to change *your* actions or thoughts, not any other person). Affirmations are really one of my favorite strategies for giving myself positive messages.

Michael Duncan, before becoming the award-winning actor in *The Green Mile*, dug ditches for a gas company. While he dug ditches, he kept dreaming that he would someday be an actor. His friends even called him Mr. Hollywood! We all know that his dream came true. He believed in himself and gave himself continuous, positive messages. He shared once that his mother always said to keep his eyes on the stars and obviously he did.

When you give yourself positive messages, you will learn to love yourself unconditionally. Belief is the magic key. Believe you can. Remember The Little Engine That Could? You can too! May each of you live with a positive voice inside!

"Recipe For A Healthy Life—Pure Air, Pure Food,
Pure Water, Exercise, and most of all, happy thoughts!"
Dr. Oliver Blaker

Avoid Comparisons

"Love yourself unconditionally just as you love
those closest to you despite their faults."
Les Brown

Did anyone ever come up to you and say, "You look just like....."?
They usually name someone famous. Over the years, I have had people
tell me that I resemble Barbra Streisand. "The way you tilt your head,
move your hands when you talk, your facial expressions," those seemed
to be the most common remarks. Sometimes, people would come up to
me after a presentation and say, "Bonnie, you remind me of someone.
I can't think of who it is..." Next, they have this contemplated look on
their faces and express relief when I immediately comment, "Barbra
Streisand!" "Right," they say with excitement! I am a tremendous fan
of Ms. Streisand but the only resemblance I could ever see was that at
birth we received the same Jewish nose.

I am certain that going through life each of us has desired to be
someone else or wished we had something that someone else had. How

many times I have heard people say "I wish I were like…because they have," "I wish I could…like them," "If only I…like them."

How many times I have heard children say, "But, Mom, I need it. Everybody has it. I have got to have it!" Many really believe that in order to feel worthy, successful, or whatever label of adequacy you want to put on it, this desired item is needed.

Those times, when we were in the comparing mode, I wondered if we really compared the whole person, the whole situation, or just the part we liked? I believe that when we would take stock of those whom we wished to model, our perspectives would change. Why, I feel certain that there are times when we all compared ourselves to the famous Joneses only to find out that somewhere, somehow, the Joneses would love to have what we have.

In the past, I would often say as people would remark on my likenesses to Ms. Streisand, "I wish I was her. I'd love to be able to sing, etc." One time as I was getting ready to give my usual response, something happened. I just stopped right in the middle of the usual remark and smiled. I really did not want to be her. I began to reflect on what I had. At the time she did not have a successful marriage and I am proud to have a very successful one. I was singing in my temple's choir; not like Barbra would have sung by any means, but I was happy to be among the participants. So what if I was not as perfect as the next in any category that I chose for comparisons? I loved what I did professionally and was grateful for all the positive differences I had come to realize that I made in people's lives. I really was and continue to be happy being me. As much as I cared about her, I did not want to be Barbra or anyone else. I was especially glad to be me.

I once heard parents sharing their intimate feelings when they were told that their first-born child was an infant with Down's syndrome. The parents openly admitted that they were not prepared for such a diagnosis and they were so scared. They spent their days imagining the worst. A neighbor shared, "This will be the biggest challenge of your lives." The parents faced each mountain head on and grew to be successful at overcoming most of their obstacles. They learned to spend their time reflecting only on what their child could do and did not compare her to others. The child began to blossom. One of the dad's final comments was the if he had to do it all over again and could choose any baby in the nursery, in a minute he would choose his daughter above all the rest.

My husband and I were taking a brisk morning walk along the boardwalk at the beach during the winter season. We walked all the way from the end of the boardwalk where our hotel was located down the strip of boards to the very beginning of the boardwalk. We had a leisurely breakfast and then began our return trip to our hotel. The air had gotten much nippier and our sense of providing ourselves with an early morning healthy activity was fast becoming a decision that was losing its value. That same distance that we had just traveled a few hours before seemed much longer. Had they extended the boardwalk while we were in the restaurant? Was it the extra poundage that we had put on our bodies while devouring our delicious breakfast? Whatever it was, our stride was much slower and the task to complete our hike appeared much more tedious. Would we ever reach our goal?

About halfway to our destination, my husband found a stone. He started to kick it along our path as we continued the cold walk. The stone had rolled over to my side and I began kicking it back to him. Before long, we were playing hockey as we took turns to maneuver that rock the remainder of our way. Before we knew it, we had reached our destination. He commented that there must be some significance to what we had just achieved and immediately shared these thoughts. "It's much easier to reach a goal when you break it down into little steps and concentrate on one little part at a time. Do your best and before long, you will realize that the overwhelming task has been completed." We recognized that we were not in competition with anyone else. People passed us by on the boardwalk but we did not mind. Accomplishing our goal was our focus. Comparing ourselves to others was not an issue.

We all have desires and goals for our families and ourselves. Let us not judge each of our worthiness by what we can or cannot do, by what we have or have not. Let us not compare ourselves by the gifts of others. Each of us has so many gifts. Let us just recognize our gifts, our efforts, our attempts, and our journey. Let us recognize and appreciate them as we continue to grow as human beings.

I read recently about the power of saying thank you, especially at a time when things seem very dark. The theory was that the more you openly expressed thanks for what you had the more your blessings you seemed to receive in your life. Not so long ago I was about to have my first experience with surgery in a hospital other than to have children. One of the strategies that I utilized in order to prepare for a positive experience was to play a thank you game with Alan on the way from our home to the hospital. We shared with each other reasons we were thankful. Some were major and some seemed frivolous by comparison. By the time I was about to enter that hospital for the very first time, for a very big female surgery, my anxiety level had been more than greatly reduced. I was recognizing and concentrating on how much I had to be thankful for in my life.

I once heard this story by Rabbi Ezekiel. It really seems so appropriate for this hug. It seems there was this rabbi who lay weeping on his deathbed. His students could not understand his actions. "Why, Rabbi," they said, "surely you will be assured a place in heaven. Why continue to cry?" The rabbi said that he was worried. He knew that when he approached the gates of heaven and was asked why he was not like Moses, he would say, "Because I was not born to do what Moses was born to do." He continued, "If I am asked why I was not Elijah, I would say, I was not born to do what Elijah was born to do." The only question I fear is that if I would not be able to answer this, "Why was I not a Rabbi Ezekiel?"

Each of us comes to this world with so many wonderful talents. Like snowflakes, each of us is alike in someway, yet in many ways we are so different.

Let us see beauty in our differences as well as our similarities. Let us appreciate those similarities and differences in ourselves as well as others. Let us find blessing in this hug.

"Of all the judgments we pass on life…
none is as important as the one we pass on ourselves."
Nathaniel Brandon

Snowflake
by Barbara Meislin

We are each of us a snowflake
No two of us the same
Reflections of the ever loving source from which we came
Unique in form and beauty, crystallized at birth
Little flecks of heaven born to melt into the earth.

We are each of us a snowflake
Of infinite design
Transitory dancers on the windowpanes of time
Unique in form and beauty, no two of us the same
Reflections of the ever loving source from which we came.

We are each of us a snowflake
A falling star in flight
A traveler through the universe, in search of our own light
Unique in form and beauty, of infinite design
Transitory dancers on the windowpanes of time.

Acknowledge Mistakes

"Failure is just a way for our lives to show us we're moving in the wrong direction, that we should try something different."
Oprah

Are there times in your overcrowded days that you wished you were a small child again? Are there times when you wished you had those frequent nurturing experiences that made you feel safe and secure when you were that small child?

Recently, I saw a toddler spill her milk on the kitchen floor. She was trying to be independent as she grabbed hold of the arm of the plastic cup. When the cup approached her mouth, the tip missed her lips, and the milk began to dribble down. Feeling frustrated and disappointed, the child dropped the cup, spilling the entire contents on the floor. When she began to cry, her mom quickly came to her rescue. The child was embraced and softly reassured that it was okay. It was just an accident. We all make mistakes. Her mother filled the cup again, gave it to the toddler, and lovingly stated, "Let's try again!"

It is easy for most individuals to recognize and exclaim that a young child is far from perfect. At the same time, it is easy for most individuals to continue to give an abundance of encouragement to that young child at each inch of development without imposing timelines. However, it is not easy for people in other stages of development (even through the senior years) to be given the same consideration. As adults, we need added boasts of cheer because many times we have created daily goals that are often insurmountable. We feel pressure to be perfect at each.

I am ready to offer words of support and encouragement to others in need. I can be heard to say, "It is okay. Everything serves. Must be a reason. Try it again. Look at what you did accomplish. How can I help? You can do it." My all-time favorite saying is, "It was not meant to be!" It seems while I am the ever-ready heartbeat for others, I cannot get to the point of giving myself the same permission for being less than perfect. At times, my version of perfect for myself would mean just to be okay.

My friend who just became a parent shared different techniques she was performing for her baby's outstanding development. She was playing classical music for him, massaging his body, and reading books together even though he could barely hold his head up. I began to reflect on how remiss I was as a parent. My husband and I had not known about this when our children were infants. What had our kids missed? Had they missed the golden windows of opportunity for success in life? Had we missed the chance to inspire our children? What we had done was to do the best job at our task with the knowledge and skills we had. When we knew more, we did more.

That is a message I believe many parents and guardians need to hear and absorb. If you are a caregiver, please use the following sentence as a mantra for the times you seem to be giving yourself an abundance of negative messages about your parenting skills. "We do the best we can with the skills and knowledge we have. When we know more we will do more."

If we believe life is a journey and we are here to enjoy it, we must then believe there will be bumps and roadblocks to pass through. We need to recognize them, learn from them, and then move forward. Helen Keller taught us to keep our face in the sunshine so we will not see the shadow.

A young man I knew took part in a camping experience for leaders in his school. There were many feats that the group of high school students had to accomplish. At the end of the session, a leader was chosen among all the teammates who had finished first in all the activities.

A young man I did not know won the award. The instructor asked this individual to share some thoughts with the group. This young man stood before his peers and announced that he was not really the leader of the team. He had made a mistake. He signaled out the young man that I knew as being the real leader. This individual went on to share how a real leader helps others achieve. "I was too interested in being number one and not considering the others," he stated. He declined the award, stating over and over again how he had made a mistake, learned from the experience, and was ready to move forward with new insights on the meaning of quality leadership.

Mistakes are going to be made by all of us as we are involved with living. It is how we grow as a result of experiencing these mistakes that will determine how we can receive this hug.

A pessimist sees a mistake as something that affect his whole life, every single avenue of his being. An optimist sees the mistake as one part of his life and is eager to brainstorm how to move forward. I consider one of my friends to be the world's biggest optimist. You can always find her stating as a problem arises, "Let's get on with it." Her enthusiasm to see the problem as a challenge and not as a life-threatening situation encourages all of us to work together to find a solution. Our feelings of being total failures are eliminated.

Another dear friend once stated that when you need to eat an elephant (tackle a big problem), just take one small bite at a time.

Here is a strategy for acknowledging our mistakes without placing ourselves in a total devastation mode.

A. Accept the mistake.
B. Brainstorm solutions.
C. Choose one to try.
D. Do it.

E. Evaluate your outcome.
F. Forge ahead if the original plan is successful.
G. Go back to brainstorming if needed.

If we were on a train traveling from Baltimore to New York and we heard the conductor shout, "Richmond, Virginia, next stop," we would realize we had made a mistake. More than likely, we would get off the train and check how we could return to our first destination. Perhaps we would have to rearrange our lives for a short time but we would get to New York. Would we be uncomfortable with the change? Probably. They say that only a baby with a wet diaper likes change, but as my friend would say, "Let's get on with it!"

If I stomped on a one hundred dollar bill, if it was dirty, or if it was old and wrinkly, would it still be worth one hundred dollars? I would certainly take it and feel certain you would, too. A mistake is a mistake, that's it. Most are not the kind that will bring devastation to us or to our world forever.

In the children's verse, "The Itsy Bitsy Spider," regardless of how much rain came down the spout, of how many times his home was washed way, the spider continued to go up the water spout. He might have made a mistake in spinning his web in that spot. However, he needed a home and he tried over and over again to move forward and correct his mistakes. The spider remained determined and committed to achieving his goals.

Just like that spider, remember that no matter what our mistake, we are still a worthwhile person, and that we can move forward, overcome, and achieve success. By acknowledging our mistakes, we can obtain that safe, secure, nurturing feeling that we once had as a baby. We can give it to ourselves!

"What is defeat? Nothing but education,
nothing but the first step towards something better."
Wendell Phillips

Stretch Out of Comfort Zones

"You can if you think you can."
Norman Vincent Peale

Do you ever hear of an island called "Someday Isle"? This island is referred to in the book, *The Magic of Masterminding*. It seems this island is where many individuals want to go one day in order to accomplish some of their goals. You probably have heard people comment that "Yes, Someday Isle…"and they state something that they would like to do. They seem to wait for that trip to "Someday Isle" before beginning to take any action. It just never seems to come!

A very bright little girl was getting ready to get into the bath that her mom had prepared for her. Being very curious, she began to watch two little fish that were in the bowl not far from her tub. She watched the fish go around in circles, the same small circles, over and over again. The little girl began to feel sad that they only had this area in which to play. So being a kind and helpful person, she dropped the fish in the tub full of water. Surely they would be happier there!

The fish seemed to be in shock as they hardly moved. I guess they never saw such a large fish bowl. At first, the little fish continued to swim in the same circumference that they had been used to in their old home. Gradually, they became braver, and began to increase the size of their play area. Before long, they were happily swimming all around the perimeter of the bathtub. The little girl's push made the fish step out of their comfort zone and see the big world. The story has a happy ending. The fish were now happy in their new environment and the little girl did not have to take a bath that night!

On the serious side, it seems as if sometimes, someone has to give us a push before we take the risk of trying something new. I know that it is not easy to step out of a comfort zone. For some, it becomes somewhat easier to shift our acquired thinking after we recognize that others have a problem. Our own emotions seem to diminish as our desire to help increases. I have just given the answer to the question many have asked of me. Why are you writing this book? The simple answer is because of others.

Please allow me to share some history of how *12 Ways To Hug Yourself* came to be. The title comes from the very first presentation I ever gave. Where did that come from? I am not certain. There are lots of incredible things that happen to me as I journey through life and I do not know how or why they occur. Rather than go into a spiritual dialogue, I will just say they do and I follow.

At the completion of my talks, people would automatically come up to me and want to hug. It was almost as if I was able to help them become free to express themselves. They did not hug their buddies or their neighbors. They came to the front of the room and would just hug me. Their reactions went from sharing, "Can I give you a hug? I just want to hug you," to just silently giving me a great hug!

Many expressed a desire to have my comments written down to review again at home as well as to share them with others. My first thought was, *Right. Sure. Me write a book? Maybe someone else could but certainly not me. No! Not Me!*

Then as the requests became numerous, I began to give the idea some thought. *Could I? Would I?* I was really scared that it would not be good enough for someone to read. *Who am I to have something this special to share with the world? Are there special degrees for this project? What gift do people see in me that I do not see in myself?* One of my children once said to me, "I wish you could see yourself as others see you." I guess I didn't.

When I received the last request, I felt this strong push that eventually became a desire that turned into a passion to create a book for my audiences. I began to talk about it. "Oh I am writing a book." As I would say those words I would laugh out loud. I'd practice saying them in front of the mirror with great expression as if I had won the Pulitzer Prize. After saying it many times over, I really started to believe I could do it (that is what happens when you give yourself many injections of positive messages).

Slowly, oh so slowly, I began to write. I was as unsteady as a child on a two-wheel bike who for the first time was riding without training wheels. I kept thinking how I promised others that I would complete this task. They had a concern and I, as a nurturer, wanted to help. My final push to step out of my comfort zone was the inspiration I received as a result of seeing those individual faces in my mind and hearing their words.

Can I write a book? I am not certain, but I am doing my best. I am scared at each step, loving the process, amazed at myself, and growing, growing and growing! Does it hurt to step out of a comfort zone? To be honest, at times, I think it does. However, with the indicators I just shared, I guess I just realized I could say, "I was successful!" For me, the success really comes in the journey. The finished product is an extra marvelous gift.

The question I find myself asking is "Why can't I stretch out of a comfort zone for myself? Why can't I take that guitar lesson just for me and take the art classes just for me?" As one of my teachers taught me to say, "You have to ASK in order to GET." Why does my spark to begin have to be someone else's reason? What is my fear? I bet you are a lot like me and share some of these same feelings.

Many of us are afraid of a change. We fear we may have to give something up if we take a risk. That change might hurt us is another phobia. We build up a tremendous defense as to why we do not need to stretch out of that comfort level. We even give ourselves a million and one reasons why we do not have to begin and therefore, we don't! Are we still going to wait for that trip to Someday Isle? Let us remember that the universe is waiting for our actions so we can be rewarded.

During a workshop the presenter defined fear as Fantasized-Experiences-Appearing-Real. Many of the fearful scenarios we embedded in our mind never really come true. However, they certainly were very strong, very real emotions at the time they were present in our thoughts.

Here are some techniques that friends and I have used that have helped us develop emotionally as we tacked new challenges and old issues.

In my opinion, an important means for stepping out of comfort zones is to practice the two hugs, Give Yourself Positive Messages and Avoid Comparisons. Since they have been discussed previously, I will just name them at this time.

Write a list of people who are able to do what you would like to do and make them your role models. The next time you are in a situation that is most uncomfortable, think about how your role model for that situation would act. Pretend you are that person and adopt that behavior. As my friend would say, "Fake it til you make it."

I often watched my granny do something that I so wished I could do. She instantly empowered people. My granny worked at a national department store for thirty-eight years. At times, I believed she thought she owned it! Many of her coworkers became like family to her. During my high school and college days, I too worked at this store.

I remember one Saturday afternoon, Granny and I were going to the cafeteria for lunch. The elevator stopped on the floor before the lunchroom and a cleaning lady entered. She had her hair tied up in scarves, a wash bucket on wheels with a mop at her side, and she wore an apron that was tattered and filled with spots. The lady smiled when she saw Granny. "Hi, Miss Rose." Granny turned to me and stated, "This is my good friend." She proceeded to give her a hug.

I can vividly remember almost every detail from that scene. My granny had so empowered that woman and made her feel very special. I have often reflected on the good feelings that were exchanged in that little space. It did not cost my granny anything to esteem her buddy. Yet I felt she gave the cleaning lady a gift of a lifetime.

She empowered me as well. I saw and felt the power of her kind words and her hug. Over the years and with much practice, I have become comfortable with trying to esteem others like Granny did as well as hug unconditionally. I hope I will always be able to achieve the same results that she did. I know that she is smiling now as I write this. I can almost hear her say, "Bonnela, only you, Bonnela!"

Another technique is to visualize what it is you want. See yourself achieving it. Keep that positive picture in your head. Many athletes have expressed using this method in reaching their athletic feats.

One of my children was taking the GMATS exam to enter graduate school. There were times during the studying for the exam when frustration set in. I asked my child to visualize a number to achieve and concentrate on that symbol. The technique worked and the number appeared as the test was scored. We were all shocked but it taught a lesson on the power of visualization of changing paradigms and stepping out. You never know what can happen.

I will often use this technique on an airplane. When the ride gets full of turbulence (heaven help the people sitting next to me), I visualize where I want to be at the end of the trip. Most often the disturbance has occurred at the end of my travel. I picture my husband waiting for me at the gate. It works! I get through the rough spots in the flight, and my neighbors on the plane do not need a tranquilizer!

Think of a mantra, sentence, and/or song to get your mind off the perceived rough spots of the challenge. At times, I have had a weak stomach with cramp-like pains in my side. I will sing the song "It's A Small World After All" (I am not certain why I chose this song), concentrating until the pains subside or I can find a more comfortable place. More times than not, due to my concentrating on the words from the song, my discomfort will disappear.

As I began writing this book, I wrote an affirmation to place in front of my workspace. Whenever I hit one of places where I am wondering what I will share next, I look at the affirmation and read it for a few times. It states, "I am gratefully rejoicing that God and I are creating *12 Ways To Hug Yourself* and it is fabulous!" I found myself getting recharged from the statement, did not concentrate on the difficulty, and continue pursuing my dream.

Life is like a kaleidoscope. One thing can happen, and all aspects of our lives are changed. We need to be able to find ways to meet these challenges and overcome them.

I was so excited to become the child care specialist of my school system but I had to learn the computer. That was a time that I can remember when it was necessary for me to step out of my comfort zone and achieve this goal for myself. I had a lot of support from my coworkers but I feel proud at last to state, "I did it." Yes, the computer and I are now friends and creating a better relationship all the time.

To conclude this chapter, I would like to share a wonderful story told to me by my dear friend. The minister was reading a book to his grandson. "Grandfather, I am so smart, " he said.

"Yes, you are," stated the minister.

The young boy looked up at his grandfather and said, "I know how much two and two are," as he raised his fingers to show the amount. Before the minister had a chance to reply, the boy shouted, "Four."

"Why that was wonderful," said the minister.

The little boy stated, "And I know how much five and five is," raising his hands again to show the total of the equation. The minister continued to play the role of the astonished professor who was just so amazed at this genius.

This game continued for quite some time, each obviously enjoying the other's company. The little boy got very serious for a moment and said, "I know how much six and six are but I need two more fingers to tell you the answer."

We have the eternal power to step out of a comfort zone when the need arises. We can do it! Let's do it now and not wait for the trip to Someday Isle. I can see you flying. Go for it! I'm proud of you!

"You have brains in your head. You have feet in your shoes.
You can steer yourself in any direction you choose."
Dr. Seuss

"When we are no longer able to change a situation
we are challenged to change ourselves."
Victor Frankel

Practice C+A=R

*"You must want to fly so much that
you are willing to give up being a caterpillar."*
Trina Paullus

What does the equation C+A=R mean? I can almost visualize you looking at those letters and saying those exact words. This alphabetical formula stands for Circumstance Plus Action Equals Response. This is a formula based on a strategy that I learned at a conference and it has greatly impacted my life.

Please allow me to share a story that will represent the significance of those letters to the quality of our daily lives. This story is about my very dear friend who was trying to conquer lung cancer. One Friday evening I was at my temple for a Shabbat service. My husband was to join me. He entered the chapel late and stated that we had to leave. I could tell by the look on his face that something was very wrong.

While we walked to our cars, Alan shared the horrifying news that he had just received. One of our closest friends had called and stated that his wife had been diagnosed that afternoon with lung cancer. My feet just buckled under me. Why, I could not believe it! We were a team. For over thirty-six years we had been great buddies who shared life together. Shocked with grief, my husband and I kissed goodbye and immediately left to be by the sides of our friends. Alan went to the workplace of her husband and I went to be with her at her home.

From the moment I walked up her steps and heard her voice, I began to assume a new role in our relationship. I was now going to be a leading actress in one of the saddest events I had ever experienced. I felt that I would certainly achieve the Best Actress of the Year Award because it was going to be the ultimate tough part and at the same time one that was most important.

My personal goal was for my friend to have the spirit and the energy to fight and conquer this dreaded enemy. My script was the same on every page, every day. "You will get over this. That's normal. This will pass. Drink, Drink, Drink! Tomorrow will be better. Eat, Eat, Eat! No, I do not think you are going to die."

In an emergency, I am really not the person you would choose to have with you. I freeze and then I lose it. I just get so scared. However, in this situation, I knew I could not do that. I had to be there for her. I had to remain positive to keep her focused on moving ahead with hope. "I can't do this. I am going to die," she would often say to me. After her negative statements, I usually commented, "Do you want to get better?" I tried to believe that if she believed it, we could somehow make her better. I can still hear her responses to me after so much frustration and desperation, "Bon, I'm trying to be positive. I want to live." This experience was a life test for my buddy and a personal test for me.

I was able to implement C+A=R into my behavior and attitude in regards to my friend's situation. Anita's cancer was the Circumstance. The Result I wanted to obtain would be based on my Actions. I had to stay focused on the positive actions, keep my feet grounded and move forward. That was how I planned to reach my Result. The date I originally wrote this chapter was February 12, 2001. Anita still had cancer, was still fighting and I was still maintaining my A for accomplishing my R. Some days, it was easy. Many times it was very difficult.

I rewrote this chapter once again in January 2002. I needed to share that my friend had succumbed to her disease. I feel so proud that I was able to be a part of her last days, providing support, hope, and love. I am so grateful that I had learned this equation to focus on as an anchor during this very sad time in my family's life.

A reality check is that C+A=R is probably easier to practice in times of sickness. My mom was able to practice this formula right after facing a life-threatening illness. When hearing the news about a tree falling on her car, her immediate response, to the amazement of everyone was, "Thank goodness no one was hurt. It is only a car." She made a conscious effort to limit the worrisome, stress messages that she would place in her body after having been informed that a reoccurrence might occur from stress-related problems.

I believe it is still easier to practice C+A=R when your result is based on a goal for someone else. Please stop a minute and reflect how it can make a difference in your everyday life from rather small circumstances to immense C's. Some examples might be: someone hurts your feelings; you are given a new aspect of your job and you have too much on your plate already; you are upset with the child's teacher and you wanted to receive another message other than the one you did receive. The C is a given. We must learn to focus on the R, the result, in order to determine our A, our action. It is the response that will ultimately determine if we get our desired results.

I remember one time I was preparing for a big Passover Seder. I was expecting twenty-eight people for a sit-down meal. My husband and children always helped me with the beginning preparations of the dinner. This time, they had very busy schedules, and did not ask me ahead of time if I needed any assistance. Feeling overburden from my own hectic schedule, I began feeling disappointed, hurt, and even somewhat angry about the lack of participation up-front. *When I will see them, I will tell them*, I thought. As I went by the refrigerator, the C+A=R magnet caught my attention.

I began to reflect on the meaning of that equation and the significance it had for the moment I was experiencing. I really wanted to have a marvelous holiday and dinner. I knew I would therefore have to change my response to this event. I never said one word to anyone. In fact, the children will probably first hear of this story as they read this chapter. During and after the dinner, my children, as usual, were wonderful holiday angels. Without my asking, they immediately helped serve and clean up. They even participated in more than expected activities. I know if I had implemented my original actions I would not have achieved this marvelous result. To this day, my children and, of course, my terrific husband pitch in to make every occasion wonderful by giving 100% or more of their effort.

To conclude our C+A=R hug, I want to share a story that I feel magnificently describes the effects this formula. A teenager, after a difficult day, was feeling very depressed. She was not selected for the team. "Everybody else got it. It was not fair." On and on she dialogued to her father about this experience. This scene could have been played out in many households across America. Here is how this father chose to finalize this moment.

Her father asked her to come into the kitchen, as he wanted to share something. Reluctantly she appeared. The father placed a carrot, an egg, and some coffee beans into separate pots filled with water. The items boiled for 20 minutes. The daughter was most impatient and continued to question her dad's intentions. At the conclusion of the boiling process, the father placed the soft carrot, the hardboiled egg, and the coffee into separate bowls on the kitchen table.

"What did you see?" he asked his daughter.

"Why? You know!" she stated as she gave him that familiar teenage look for "Really!" She eventually responded in a loud and disgusting voice, "A soft carrot, a hardboiled egg, and some coffee."

The father said, "This, my daughter, is what you are seeing. Each of these items have been exposed to 20 minutes of boiling (the C=Circumstance) but they each acted (the A=Action) differently. The carrot became soft and mushy as a result of the experience. The egg became hardened on the outside from the same event. The result from the coffee beans was much different. They had the same experience happen, but they became enriched by the circumstance. They were not softened by it or hardened by it. Their actions were deliciously right!" They became better from having gone through the experience.

I practice C+A=R on a daily basis. Some days, some times, it is not so difficult. Other days and times it is a battle. My goal is to make it a natural part of my existence and I am a work in progress. Following this equation is one way I believe we can provide ourselves with a quality life. Remember, we cannot control the events in our lives, only our responses. Let us determine what outcomes we will choose for ourselves so we can share in a wonderful journey called life.

I have passed this "ah ha!" formula on to my family, friends, and participants in my classes and workshops, hoping that it will make them have a more happier, fulfilling life. My wish for you, as Mikey's brother said, "Try it, you'll like it!"

"It is not because things are difficult that we do not dare.
It is because we do not dare that they are difficult."
Lucas Nannies Seance

Recognize Successes

"The attitude you take towards problems and difficulties is far and away the most important factor in controlling and mastering them."
Norman Vincent Peale

Can you name one hundred successes that occurred before you were 18? Difficult? Okay, could you name twenty? A group of people at a seminar was asked those questions. Individuals began to shuffle in their seats and look around the room. The expression denoting, "This has got to be a joke," seemed to appear on many faces. I know it was on mine. I began to think of what I had accomplished that was so great. I did have the privilege of becoming the Baltimore County Teacher of the Year and a finalist for Maryland in 1992. That was a terrific, fabulous achievement. However, I could not think of one before age 18. Surely, I was successful at something during those years. I could not find an answer to that question. From discussions later, others in the group had the same problem.

Think about these following examples for the answer: learning how to eat, lift our heads, walk, talk, drive, sing, jump, play a game, etc. They are successes. The participants had looked upon them as goals that everyone achieved, and were searching for the gold accomplishment to acknowledge. Many of us can now think of other individuals that cannot reach those feats due to having some disability. Perhaps after reading this, we will take time to reflect with gratitude on the one hundred and more such goals we can accomplish and see them as successes.

A dear friend had been trying to start a family of her own. She was a classroom teacher and for years her students were like her children. Finally, her dream was coming true. When she was with child, the entire school became excited with the new baby coming into our world. Six months into the pregnancy, she gave birth to Baby Jessie. Due to many insurmountable problems, the child only lived for six hours.

What a loss this was for a family who had so much love to give! The parents shared that they were planning to have a memorial service for Jessie. Reviewing the past such services I had attended, I was not certain if I would be expected to say a few words. As I was driving with one of my children, I expressed that I somehow wanted to find a positive message to share with everyone at this time.

There was silence in the car. Then my child stated, "Think about how successful the baby was even though he only lived for such a short time." I could not understand that statement. My child continued, "Baby Jessie had touched so many lives in a positive way; all the boys and girls, their families, the school personnel. Think about how much happiness he brought his parents and how the process of his development and birth had strengthened their marriage. Some people feel that you are a success when you make a difference in another person's life. Baby Jessie made lots of them. I would say Baby Jessie was a successful person, regardless of the time he lived." That is a message that I carried with me to the service, shared with friends, and continue to save in a special place in my heart.

The yardstick for measuring success need only be our personal one defined by our standards. I think our failures become abundant when we allow other individuals to determine how we should feel. Everyone has a basic need for being successful. Recognizing the effort or the journey of a task as a success, I believe, is a great technique for achieving this hug. The writing of this book, from conception of the project through the process until the writing of the last chapter, has given me a wonderful sense of achievement. When the book is published and it becomes a great hit, the feeling of success will probably be even sweeter. I am not waiting for the final step to enjoy the fruits of my labor. I am tasting it all the way up (please note how I stated the above in words that will send me a positive message).

Another problem with our being able to recognize a personal success is that society seems to give us permission to tell only a tale of woe. The stories denoting jubilation of our triumphs are looked upon as a means of bragging.

Well, Will Rogers said, "If it is the truth, it is not bragging."

For an icebreaker, I asked a group of teachers to share a good story about themselves and or their class. There was complete silence and then some exhibited signs of uneasiness that was easily detected from their body language.

I then modeled and slowly they felt comfortable to speak on the topic. I shared their group reactions at the conclusion of their limited comments. I stated that I felt if I had asked them to share a concern or negative story I knew they would all be eager to speak. I have seen this occur from past experiences. They all laughed and nodded in agreement.

Try some of the following enriching activities as a means for the celebration of your accomplishments.

A. Give yourself permission to write a list of things that you really like about yourself. Keep the list handy in order to refer to it whenever necessary. We all have those unsettling moments when we need to remind ourselves how terrific we are. Go for it!

B. Place a picture of a hand on a wall (if this is impossible, keep the picture somewhere within easy reach). Each time you feel you have achieved something noteworthy by your standards, go over to the poster and rub your back on the hand. This is your own "Pat on the Back Machine." Why wait for others? Appreciate yourself and do so as many times as you want. It sounds funny, but it makes you smile and lifts up esteem.

C. Stand in front of a mirror at the end of the day and share all the tasks you felt need recognition. Recognize them with great, positive emotions (in order to avoid any misunderstanding, please notify your family ahead of time as to what it is that you are doing).

D. Keep a victory journal. The beauty of this activity is that as you reread those memories, you immediately obtain affirmative feelings. At times, we may have a feeling of being stuck in a place in our lives that keeps us from moving forward. These written notes can become the motivation to begin again.

At the writing of this chapter, I am feeling an extraordinary sense of pride over two of my very recent successes. I will have the privilege of going before the Torah to become a Bat-Mitzvah at the end of this year. Part of my preparation for this Jewish ceremony is for me to relearn the Hebrew language. I went to Sunday School and was confirmed when I was young. However, that saying "If you don't always use it, you can lose it" applies in my situation. In the past, I could follow some of the Hebrew prayers due to memory. If I had to read a portion I was at a lost. For the past several months, I have studied the Hebrew language and have now started to become knowledgeable about the chanting of the prayers. Yes, I am so busy, but I am also feeling a strong sense of personal pride at each moment of success in this endeavor. I am savoring each moment and eagerly share my feelings and accomplishments with my family and friends.

The second success that I am proud to share is the acceptance of my two stories for inclusion in the book, *Chicken Soup for the Teacher's Soul*. In 1992, I had the privilege of hearing the authors describe how the book was conceived and heard the tales of its journey for completion.

Due to that experience, I have taken a personal interest and delight in the success of the series.

Five or six years ago, I decided to write two stories "What a Great Answer" and "Why Choose Teaching?" for possible inclusion into a book of this type for teachers. This will probably sound weird, but as I was writing the words, I could feel that I was creating a golden message to be shared. This feeling stayed with me during the entire process of completing this task.

I sent my writings to the authors. I received a letter stating that these stories had possibilities for consideration for the book. I filled in a questionnaire that they also sent, returned the letter, and become involved in other life events. Shortly thereafter, a message came that the book was on hold. Life goes on!

Several months ago, I received a letter announcing that my stories were part of the final 200 out of 5,000 to be considered for the book. My husband, children, and especially myself were so very excited. Then the evening arrived that I received another letter from the Chicken Soup family. It was a thick one, something on the size of a college acceptance note. One of my children was with me at the time I received this mail. We automatically began to dance and state, "What if?" but we never finished the statement. As I read the words of acceptance aloud, our cheers, dancing, and jumping became abundant. This indeed was a dream come true! It is difficult for me to put into words all the wonderful feelings I am having as a result of that acceptance.

As I am editing this book once again, rereading this chapter makes me feel great. I now am able to recognize so many successes in my life—those that I accomplished on my own and those that I accomplished with the help of others. I am proud and grateful for each one. I hope we meet one day where we can share our successes with each other.

Having obtained the feeling of success is a special, personal blessing and hug. May each of us have the ability to recognize our achievements, regardless of size, during our journey.

"Failure is success if we learn from it."
Malcolm S. Forbes

Be a Miracle Detective

"There are only two ways to live your life. One is as though nothing is a miracle. The other is as though everything is a miracle."
Albert Einstein

What is a miracle? In my presentations, I have asked participants to define that question. For many, the meaning proved difficult to explain. When the reluctant responses began to emerge, similarities were noted. However, as individuals' life experiences differed, so too did the answers.

Several years ago my good friend and I created a self-esteem/social skills program for children and parents called HUGS. Various structures of families prevalent in today's society participated. During one of the beginning implementations, I asked the group that same question, "What is a miracle?" I waited for a reply. After what seemed like an appropriate period of time for the answer, I began to feel that perhaps I was not going to have any explanation from the individuals. To my excitement, one dear little boy raised his hand and exclaimed with pride, "I know what a miracle is. It was a miracle that my grandmother's trunk stayed opened!" We all began chuckling as we imagined the scene he was referring to at home. A wonderful discussion on the various miracles in life then ensued. The topics went from the simple, "Jim is sitting still," to the complex "And my mom is well again."

Each week of the program the children arrived and responded to that question in their journals. Some of their entries were, "My miracle was my pottery broke but I didn't cry. I just thought of a different use for it." "I got my spelling words all right without looking at the chart." "The girls in the class liked me today." One little fellow stated, "It was a miracle that I got recess today!" And it was!

At a holiday sermon much before September 11, 2001, my rabbi stated "our country is at its greatest, yet we have so many unhappy people." After reading David Elkind's remarks that "children are dying of stress-related illnesses," and having recalled my own previous experiences, I recognized how important it was to discover ways to create personal happiness beginning from the inside.

I believe that this hug is one strategy that has the power to accomplish that goal. Opening ourselves to the wonders that happen in our own world every day enables us to find an abundance of miracles (good things) in our daily lives. We need to begin by practicing the recognition of positive occurrences, the labeling of them first to ourselves and then sharing such events with others. Our children, our families, and most importantly, ourselves, will begin to fully realize how many miracles happen to us. The events are not to be counted by the size or by their impact but rather that they just simply occurred.

I implemented the same HUGS program at two homeless shelters. The curriculum was altered to meet the needs of the adults. When we came to the session that discussed this HUGS, the participants grew very quiet. "Miss Bonnie, there are not any miracles in my life. Do you know what troubles I have?" Then, each in turn repeated a sorrowful, personal tale.

I listened with great empathy and concern. When they seemed to have come to a pause, I asked them to close their eyes. They responded and I proceeded to give them my next request. "Please take a moment and think about the steps you were required to do in order to get out of bed this morning." We then listed actions they had taken to accomplish that goal: open your eyes, breath, turn your bodies around, sit up, etc. Next, I asked the group to close their eyes once again, and picture a blind person performing that same action. How were his actions the same or different than theirs?

From that experience, the participants began to rattle off "miracles" that happen to them on a daily basis. Their esteem began to blossom for the moment. By the time our class was over, they seemed to have gained a spark of enthusiasm. We all hugged as we left the room with smiles on our faces and a sense of hope for a good day.

I am excited when I recognize a miracle moment in my life. I am in awe that the event even occurred. The smile on my face feels like it has gone from ear to ear in seconds. I cannot wait to share it with others. I especially look forward to sharing it with my husband and children for I want to help them to become enriched by recognizing miracles in their lives. This is a great hug!

During the last class of the children's HUGS program, I asked individuals to complete a group evaluation of the sessions. Their very first comment and one that each eagerly responded to was "we learned how to recognize miracles." I feel confident that even when the children became adults they would be able to recognize many miracles in their lives.

I try hard to focus on this skill in order for the positive behavior to become one of my habits. Over the years, I have acquired a proficiency at this technique due to my practicing every day. Consequently, it has strengthened so many areas of my life. It continues to create in me a feeling of closeness with my God and reinforces my belief that I am truly never alone.

As the children's excitement over the recognition of their miracles grew, I hope that you too will take time to reflect on your everyday miracles and grow in excitement over your recognition of them. I believe so strongly that it will bless your life forever.

"Coincidences are God's ways of staying anonymous."
Les Brown

Recreate a Treasured Memory

"Life is a kaleidoscope of beautiful moments."
Helen Keller

What is a "treasured memory"? In my summation from reviewing The American Heritage Dictionary of the English Language's definitions for the words *treasured* and *memory,* I concluded that the following meaning would be appropriate for my reflections. "A treasured memory is a recollection of things considered especially precious." Please allow me to share one of my most precious things.

I was a kindergarten teacher. Looking back on my days in that classroom, I am proud to share that I thought I was a great one. I loved my kids and their families, gave them my all, and recognize that I made a positive impact on their lives. My husband used to tell others, "Bonnie never thinks that she goes to work." That is how much I loved my job—at least 98% of the time.

After my beloved principal and mentor announced that he was moving to another position, and after crying like a baby in one of the children's cubbies, I began to reflect that perhaps it was time for me to move on. Where and what would I want to do? It seemed that for my whole life I only wanted to be a kindergarten teacher.

Truth be known, days before the principal's statements to the faculty, I had started to analyze my recent feelings of restlessness. Recognizing the gifts I brought to the families in my class, in my school, and in that community, I began to make some inquires. What were the possibilities of utilizing all my skills and successes in a larger part of the school system?

Before long, I had been approached to consider becoming an assistant principal. I can honestly say that fears and doubts began to set into my thoughts. The mantra, "Will I be good enough to do the job?" began to play in my head. With great anxiety as I was about to travel into unknown territory, with an "I Can" attitude, with many positive affirmations and unconditional support from family, friends, colleagues, and the children's parents, I accepted the challenge.

The task of packing all of my classroom materials was my first big obstacle. I looked about my kindergarten room at the things I had collected over the years that enhanced the excitement of learning for the children. Everything seemed to hold a special meaning. Oh, how lucky I was to be able to have some things that still captured those special moments: drawings, notes, letters, little trinkets, presents, books. Of course, the biggest, most satisfying presents were the memories I shared with those children and their families.

I did realize that some things would have to go. As a flea market queen and a saver of anything and everything, it was most difficult to put something in the throwaway pile. One never knew when one might need 18 white socks, all in good condition!

I decided that the very first thing I wanted and needed to pack was all of my tangible mementos that I had savored throughout my years in that classroom and school. They were my incredible roots that I wanted by my side as a sort of security blanket as I tackled my new experience. I realized that treasured memories brought about a sense of stability in uncertain times. Hence, I began stuffing a box and filling it to the brim.

In my new position, just as I had heard others state when in a new adventure of life, I imagined there would be times when I really missed my kindergarten assignment. This box was going to be a sweet reminder of days gone by, of successes of the past. This was my instant hug. Those moments did come. I found myself closing my office door and glancing at my treasured memory box. The feeling of positive self-esteem denoting that I was lovable, capable, and special surrounded me. To this day, whenever I glance at those items in my special container, I receive that same feeling.

We all go through periods of change in our lives. Some we chose. Others were given for us. I encourage each of you to create treasured memory boxes to help you recreate wonderful memories of times gone by. This special hug will help take you to a special place almost instantly.

I had a chance to create a treasured memory for my husband upon his retirement from a position he had held for 25 years. Alan was about to leave many wonderful friends behind, friends who probably felt more like family due to the amount of daily moments he spent with them. I knew this new journey would bring happiness but would also bring some sad moments as he planned to leave his dearly beloved buddies. In order for him to remember those special people, I created a collage from pictures taken at his retirement party. They are proudly displayed in his office right in front of his desk. I felt that Alan would always be able to view those pictures whenever he chose, in times when the challenges would be easy as well as those that may prove to be somewhat tougher. I knew that this treasured memory would bring him many smiles and wonderful feelings of special times.

I continue to create treasured memories for the many wonderful times Alan and I, the children and our family and friends have experienced. I even made one guest room decorated in some of my children's most beloved items. At times, I have seen them in the room and have heard conversations that are filled with joy and love as they recall a dear, happy memory.

Hug yourself by recreating ways to enjoy treasured moments. You can begin anytime. Just begin!

"The things that count most in life are the things that can't be counted."
Zig Zigler

Perform an Act of Kindness

*"We must not, in trying to think about how we can make a big
difference, ignore the small differences we can make."*
Marion Wright Edelman

Did someone do something kind for you today? If the answer is yes,
and I hope that it is, how did it make you feel? Were you able to spread
that same feeling by performing an act of kindness for someone other
than yourself today?

I believe that each of us would like to do something to make this
world a better place. Often we have lengthy discussions about such
events, but sadly, they remain only discussions without any action.
Please allow me to share some stories that will portray people acting
upon ideas to create a kinder world.

Each September, our local florist has "A Good Neighbor Day." He
gives a dozen red roses to individuals free of charge. The only
responsibility the receivers have is that eleven must be given away.
People begin lining up way before the store opens in order to take part
in this kind act. By the end of the afternoon, Mr. or Ms. Citizen had

delivered hundreds of flowers. Individuals from all walks of life have been touched by this gesture.

Over the years, the florist has shared many stories with me as told to him by recipients' letters. The following story is one of my favorites. An elderly woman was watching the news and heard the reporter describe "A Good Neighbor Day." *How I wished someone would do that for me,* she wrote to the florist. *I could have used something cheering in my life!* She did not harbor any jealous feelings about others receiving the roses. She continued to state in her letter how excited she was that so many people would be affected by such a special activity.

Sometime in the evening her doorbell rang. A woman, whom she had never seen before, extended her hand and gave the lady a present—a rose! In her letter to the florist this woman stated that she had been overcome with happiness. She had run to put it in her vase and placed it on her night table next to her most precious belonging—her rosary. That was how much worth the woman put on that act of kindness.

It is interesting to hear the owner of the flower shop speak of his original plan for that special day. He was not aware of the magnitude that this event would take on in the community. He was not aware of how many kindnesses would be performed as a result of his actions. The florist's feelings of self-worth, as well as his belief in the goodness of others, had been greatly enhanced by his plan. He used something in his environment to create a magnificent kind deed that created hugs for him many times over. How many of us would be willing to take time from our lives to create an action plan to implement for the sake of sharing kindnesses? That is the beauty of performing an act of kindness. While we perform it unselfishly for others, our life is greatly enriched.

"The fragrance of the rose lingers on the hand of the giver."
Anonymous

I was purchasing some items from a card shop one day. I was using my new, smiley face pen to write the check. The cashier stepped away from the register for a few minutes, which gave me some time to chat with the girl behind me in line. We had a delightful conversation that concluded with her sharing that she was studying to become a teacher. I felt so proud that she chose this career path. As I completed my purchase, she commented on my adorable pen. I proceeded to give it to her and shared, "I'm proud you want to become a teacher. Please take this as a gift from another teacher. If you ever get stuck in your dream, look at the pen and keep going!" She beamed and so did I. I will never know if she became a teacher, or for that matter if she even has that pen. I know she went out of that store happy. I received much personal satisfaction from that event. Even as I write about it today, I am smiling and thinking happy thoughts about the experience. Elie Wiesel wrote, "No matter how concerned you are about mankind as a whole you must never overlook the individual. Every human being is a world in himself."

Doing an act of kindness is not about the size. It may be as easy as giving a piece of candy to a co-worker who yells, "I am having a chocolate fit." It may be as simple as leaving a note for someone to read, speaking extra-kind sentiments to someone for no special reason, bringing in a special food item to share with others, or perhaps giving a star sticker to an individual for finding something that was misplaced.

In a *Family Circus* cartoon, a child and mom stood in front of the refrigerator. The mom kept asking the child what he wanted and listed many items. The child always responded to each suggestion with "No."

Finally, feeling frustrated, she stated, "Well, what do you want?" The child smiled and simply responded, "A hug." Sometimes that act of kindness is just a hug or a smile. Given at the right moment, these little kindnesses can become "the ultimate kind act."

I would be remiss if I did not share a marvelous act of kindness that was led by one man who brought hope to so many children and families. The man was Riverview Elementary School's "Uncle Marty," a local owner of several catering halls. Uncle Marty agreed to adopt the school where I was a kindergarten teacher. Following are but a few of the kindnesses he performed for everyone.

Uncle Marty gave a catered "dream" luncheon once a month for all the children who had good attendance, who raised their academic achievement, who showed great effort, and/or who had exhibited good or improved citizenship. The parents were even invited to attend. He provided the children and families with ice cream sundaes and special dinners throughout the school year to help teachers promote parent involvement. Swim parties at Uncle Marty's home, trips to amusement parks and baseball games were also provided by our hero. He encouraged the children to always do their best, stay in school, and that he would be there to help them. For over ten years, he continued to provide such acts of kindness. Why, Uncle Marty even gave our parents jobs.

There is one particular time that I wanted to share in detail. One of our instructional assistants was brutally murdered one evening after school. Everyone was in a state of shock. I called Uncle Marty at home and told him what had happened, explained how we were all hurting, and shared that we all needed him.

The next day, Uncle Marty came to school and visited every classroom sharing sentiments, listening to the students and just hugging all of our school family. Just his caring presence made a difference in the school environment. On the day of the funeral, while many school personnel attended the service, Uncle Marty came to school to be included in the long list of substitutes for the morning.

Many people had commented that he was a wealthy man, had a catering hall and could easily do all that. They missed the significance of performing acts of kindnesses. This gentleman gave more than money could ever purchase. He gave of himself over and over again. Uncle Marty touched everyone in that school and community. He has received much recognition for his outstanding contributions to our school and community. I feel certain, when reflecting on all of his awards, hearing someone say, "Hi Uncle Marty," and then receiving a hug from the individual, is probably one of his most memorable.

Let us practice looking for the moments when we can perform an act of kindness for someone. Please remember that a smile can be the easiest and often the most lasting. My friends, I hope my book will serve as an act of kindness for you.

"One thing I know: The only ones among you who are really happy are those who will have sought and found how to serve."
Albert Schweitzer

Do Something Fun

"The tragedy of life is not death,
rather it is what we allow to die within us while we live."
Norman Cousins

Is there anyone you know who doesn't like to have fun? I really do not think I know anyone like this. What I do know is that in our busy lives today, too many people, young and old, do not add "fun" to their lists of daily or weekly "to do's." Many who do never seem to accomplish that goal. Too many individuals strive every hour to be successful in numerous ways and areas of life. Even an unexpected event that could have had possibilities of fun is often dismissed due to "lack of time."

I can just imagine what some of the comments would be from those individuals sited above when someone shared about this hug: How can I fit that in? Who will go with me? I can't…because…because…because! The rational for omission goes on and on. I am convinced that it is the "fun" in life that creates a positive focus on all of our other commitments, especially that of staying mentally and physically fit.

As I am rewriting this draft (again) it is snowing outside.

How beautiful this act of nature makes my gardens look on the sometime dreary days of winter. How beautiful the inside of my home appears as a result of the snow scenes from each window. Although fresh, clean snow can make the world look magnificent, it can also create havoc on the roads.

I had an appointment this morning and the weather report was denoting the details of the upcoming storm. Knowing that I really wanted to keep this date, I convinced my husband to drive me. It would be about a 20-25 minute ride. As we were leaving the house, I packed all of our cold weather emergency clothing and apparatus needed in case of an emergency. I even packed an energy drink in case we were out alone for a long time (I did forget to pack toilet paper, an item my mother reminded me to always keep in my emergency kit).

We were laughing and smiling like little kids as we finally drove away to reach our destination. It was a fun experience. We took a situation that could have been trying and created moments of fun. That set the tone for the whole morning and would probably be carried over to the entire day.

I once worked in an office where the copy machine was always in need of repair due to the immense workload it was asked to produce. The same gentleman was always sent by the company to solve our technology problem.

Although my coworkers and I did not relish having the machine breakdown, we did enjoy the wonderful, inviting mannerisms of this gentleman. He was a ray of sunshine on any given day. I was amazed how his body language and positive comments would change the atmosphere of the office personnel. One day I asked him why he was always so happy. He responded by stating, "This is the only November 13,1997, I will ever have, so why not be happy and have fun?"

I once heard this story that demonstrates the significance of this hug. Two men were chopping wood. At the end of the day they had cut the same amount even though their work habits were different. The first man would work right through each hour of the day without taking any breaks. The second man worked hard for 45 minutes of the hour and then stopped for the last 15 minutes.

The first gentleman, who worked without taking that break, was frustrated. How could they possibly have the same amount of wood at the end of the day? What was happening? What was he doing wrong? Finally he asked the second gentleman for his secret in achieving his goal when, at times during the day, the gentleman ceased his work. The second gentleman stated that he spent those 15 minutes sharpening his saw.

I believe that is what purpose "fun" has in our lives. When sharpening our saw, by adding fun to our days, we can perform our daily tasks and live our lives more effectively.

One of my children called me on December 31 to wish me a Happy New Year. I responded immediately with, "Thanks! I know it will be a great one." My child answered my reply with, "Mom, you know how to make it fun."

It made me feel grateful and proud that I was able to create many fun times in our family's life. I continue to try and create such moments as I recognize how special those memories can be, especially when dealing with difficult events.

April 15 is a very famous date in our home. My husband is finished doing taxes for clients (there are always late patrons but, by and large, his work is completed for another year). It is a tough time in our household. Everyone is put on the second ladder as our father and husband reaches out to fulfill clients' needs. While each family member understands, at times, it is a lonely feeling. I choose to use this time for the planning of our summer vacation. It has become a family tradition. Everyone becomes very excited and eagerly offers input for our destination and agenda. This activity helps each of us maintain our focus on a happy, fun family goal during Dad's busiest time.

Each of us may have our own definition of fun. The common thread would be that it is the result of a person's attitude. Happiness is an inside job that only we can provide for ourselves. Life is too short for that negative attitude which will only diminish the fun in our life. A co-worker shared this statement: "Each of us has the ability to make our own weather regardless of the situation."

Having fun in your life can also be related to the hug "stretching out of a comfort zone." As I began my writing today, I was thinking about some of my major professional accomplishments. After reviewing several, I began to reflect how each of them began as a spark to help others. Some of them I would never have given a thought to do just for myself. As I recall the memories, the good times, and the fun associated with each, I cannot help but smile and at times laugh aloud. I can only say how glad I am that I took the step to begin (much like the writing of this book).

Someone may share an idea or event that they did and thought it was the best thing since chicken soup (the person must not have had some of my husband's). The way it was described may sound great but it would be something you would never think to experience. Then, the right moment seems to appear, the right person may share the activity using just the right words, and BINGO, you find yourself in the midst of having fun!

Let me tell you about such a moment in my life. Alan and I were on a cruise. We stopped at an island that had a nude beach. The young camper in me convinced my oh-so-straight mate to "just once in our life let's try nude swimming!" For argument's sake, I rationalized that we did not know anyone (our friends chose to remain back). So, eager me and reluctant Alan waded through the shallow water to get to the part of the beach that was strictly for unclothed bathing.

As we approached the small area, we could see couples scattered about, seemingly absorbed in their own thoughts. We quickly removed our clothing and ran in the water. It was great…so much fun! Free at last! Friends, nothing to bind you up or hold you in, just free as a bird and feeling great!!! Each of us could now understand why others had exclaimed that it was so much fun!

Then a problem occurred. A couple that we met during an activity on the cruise ship invaded our beach. Their eyes spotted ours and I am not certain as to which husband and wife team was in greater shock! I could see by my husband's expression on his face that the feelings of fun were about to fly briskly away and be replaced with a storm of words that would definitely be shared with me!

Trying to maintain my "fun" time, I began shouting as the couple approached the sand. "Let's make a deal," I said. "We will focus on the horizon until you are fully in the water. When we are ready to go back to our towels and clothing on the beach, you can return the favor." We all laughed and the pact was made. Our fun time was still on!

While we were all under the water with just our heads showing, we shared funny scenarios about what our children and friends would say. We shared stories about our lives and our dreams and we giggled and giggled and giggled. It was a terrific adventure! Towards the end of our new experience, we all made a pact not to fully share our day at the beach with others. During the remainder of the cruise, whenever our eight eyes met, we broadly smiled, winked, laughed and probably reflected on what the others' thoughts might have been.

I encourage you to take some time after reading this chapter to think about some of the things you really like to do for fun. Write them down and reflect how long it has been since you did them. Perhaps you can create a list of things you would like to do in the near future or at least begin to investigate. Some suggestions would be listen to music, read, paint, knit, meditate, join a special group that has nothing to do with your work or any other family member (I joined a choir and I am the most enthusiastic person but probably the least talented), share a joke with someone, spend time in a book store, treat yourself to something special, write in a journal, take lessons, take day trips, etc. (Of course, all the fun things would never bring embarrassment or harm to another.) See how you can create and accomplish fun in your daily and weekly schedule. Remember, we all need to sharpen our saws!

My dad died at the unthinkable early age of 29. I remember my mom sharing that he was always full of fun, never liked to be too serious, and that saving for a rainy day was not one of his major priorities. I am so grateful to know that during the short time he lived, he had fun. I hope our angels who were sent to heaven as a result of September 11, 2001, had fun before they had to so quickly leave us.

Please hug yourself by creating moments of positive fun, ones that put smiles on your face, ones that can make you laugh, and ones that make you so feel so thankful to be alive!

Remember what the copy machine man shared.

"You've got to dance like nobody's watching, love like you'll never get hurt, sing like there's nobody listening, and live like it's heaven on earth."
Unknown

Surround Yourself with Granny Roses

"Every blade of grass has its angel that bends over it and whispers grow."
Talmud

What is a Granny Rose? I bet you are probably thinking, *I never heard of that kind of flower*. It is my privilege to share what is a Granny Rose. I had a Granny Rose. She was my grandmother, my dad's mom, and an angel in my life. She extended to me unconditional love and made me feel, at all times, that I could fly. She was always boasting about my accomplishments. Sometimes they were stretched truths to the point that I did not recognize myself. I remember one special time when we were coming home on the bus from work. Granny worked at the Hecht Company for over 30 years. I worked there during high school and college. This particular evening that I am recalling we managed to get seats but they were in back of each other. I sat behind my grandmother and heard her share that I was going to be the smartest teacher and my boyfriend (now my husband of 40 years) was going to be the best accountant—so smart they are! I remember giggling about those remarks but feeling so proud at the same time. There was so much love included in her words and her tone as she shared her feelings to the stranger in the next seat.

I could call my granny anytime and share something so insignificant or so unimportant, and she always listened. She would always respond with an affirmative word and I would hang the phone up feeling so happy. I remember leaving her hospital room in the final month of her life and standing outside the door to listen to what would be her last story about her Bonnela, her wonderful husband, and her marvelous children. You have no idea how empowering those memories remain for me today. She was truly my dream builder!

I am most fortunate to have many "Granny Roses" in my life and to be able to call upon them at any time for an unconditional loving response that I now call the Granny Rose response. With those kind of intentionally nurturing individuals in our lives, one cannot help but reach personal and professional success.

There are times when my Granny Roses reach out and hug me without an exchange of words. They make me feel nurtured, the same I would do for them. There are times when they just note how special they think I am and conclude with "I love you." These are the same sentiments I would exchange with them.

Please take time to find your Granny Roses. If you have one in your life, then you are a very lucky person. They are a most precious gift. Practice being a Granny Rose yourself. You will find that you will become a magnet to other Granny Roses and be able to develop special, quality relationships.

Here is a beautiful story as to how I modeled Granny Rose's behavior and how it made a difference in a life. It was my first time teaching a beginning childcare course at a local community college. I was so nervous, as I had not had many hours of advanced notice to prepare. When my students arrived, I could not help but take note how different each of us were: backgrounds, ages, religions, cultures. Our common goal was that we were dedicated to improving the lives of children and their families. Through our passion for others, we became sisters during that semester. We shared our hopes, our dreams, and our fears.

During one of our sessions, a member of our class family stated that she had leukemia and was in remission. All through the week, I could not stop thinking about her personal strength and her determination to live with her disease and to still reach her goal of becoming a teacher. At our second class, I gave her a pin. It read, "Miracles Happen." She tearfully accepted the present and wore it to many classes. The pin was a small catalyst for her to maintain hope.

About halfway through the semester, this individual reported to the class that she was no longer in remission. Each of us hugged her, cried, and pledged to help her in any way. We were her guardian angels during those college hours. Keeping focused on her goal, she managed to take treatments for her illness and still come to class. We indeed were her Granny Roses for fifteen weeks.

At the end of the last class, she reported that the disease had now spread and she was tired of fighting. She was ready to give up. I was devastated. I could not just let her lose hope. I shared that I heard what she was saying, that I recognized her frustration, her disappointment and sense of hopelessness. Then I began to relate how much she had to give to the world, how her presence made such a difference. I asked her to try to find some time and means of going away by herself to reevaluate her life. It was the last class, the last goodbye, the last hug that the class buddies exchanged.

On December 31 of that year, I received a letter from this student. (The letter had been written on my birthday—the day before.) She stated than she indeed had been wallowing in self-pity but that she had taken my advice. She was able to get away and do a lot of thinking. She had decided to continue the treatments at night and to apply for a job somewhere in a daycare center. Her comments continued, "If I accomplish one thing in my life it will be to make a difference in a child. Thank you so much, and the next time you have a heart talk in class, can you tell how you made a difference in my life?"

I was a Granny Rose for my student. It was contagious. With all her problems, this individual recommitted herself to becoming a Granny Rose for a child. My Granny Rose made a difference in my life. I passed the gift to another. She passed it on to still another.

Granny has been gone for many years now. Her dream building

behavior that she modeled has become a very strong part of who I am today. The journey of life is great. There are many bumps along the way. We need dream builders, the good listeners, the great nurturers, and the eternal cheerleaders to be by our side as we remove the obstacles for reaching any means of success in life.

I hope all of you will have the opportunity to find a Granny Rose and receive the responses that will surely make you blossom. May you pass it on to another. It is the greatest hug of all.

"If you have just one or two spiritual friends with whom you can share your highest aspirations you should consider yourself richly blessed."
Swami Kris Canada

Epilogue

Please allow me to share a unique time in my life where I needed to practice all my hug strategies on a daily bases. On February 21, 2001, I had major surgery. It was the first time that I was in a hospital for an extended stay except the special times when I gave birth to my three children. When I heard my doctor say "operation" I became more than surprised, to say the least, and very upset. In the past, due to my family's history, I had often equated sicknesses, hospitals, and operations with death. As intelligent as I am, there still are certain fears that seem to linger within and all it takes is something to bump the scab and the sore opens raw again.

After my initial reaction to my doctor's comments, I shared with my husband all my thoughts and feelings about this upcoming event. My vocalizations went something like this. "Well! I really know what I have to do. I am always telling others the power of positive self-talk, meditation, exercise, healthy food, and vitamin therapy. Now I have to get my act together or I will be a hypocrite." I knew it would be a tough goal. I became committed to practicing those good health techniques. Here is how the 12 Hugs played a major role in my full, outstanding, marvelous surgery and recovery.

Eat Something Forbidden

I was given instructions to eliminate my food intake after midnight on the day before surgery. The night before, I had a big dinner where I ate some of my favorite foods, including many that were fattening. I even had two ice cream drinks. The food consumed was more than I would have normally eaten in any one meal, even on a special occasion. I seemed to have given myself permission to eat whatever I desired as well as to eat how much I wanted. It was as though I thought I was never going to eat again for a year!

Give Yourself Positive Messages

Shortly after hearing my news, I had to attend a staff meeting where everyone shared "what's up" professionally in our lives. Quite often it was hard to separate the personal aspects of our daily living with our work. For me, this was one of those occasions. I knew the protocol of our sessions and found myself practicing what I wanted and needed to say to my wonderful work buddies.

Knowing I needed to give myself positive messages and knowing that I needed the support of everyone to help me live in that positive world, I shared, often through tears, the following, "I am going through some tough times with planning for my upcoming health problem and with working through the emotions felt with the recent notification of my mom's reoccurring breast cancer." I continued, "Thank you so much for all your hugs in the past, and please continue to hug me often at this time."

I further stated, "I also need something besides your physical and emotional support. I will be working very hard to maintain a positive attitude. Please avoid telling me any stories, giving me any advice from others' past experiences, or asking me any questions about either situation. Just hug me!"

They lovingly fulfilled my request. Because of their unconditional acceptance and willingness to comply with my needs, I was given the courage to ask others, in different arenas, to give me the same assistance. I actually asked for what I needed, without feeling guilty, or without having the need to find a way to give back to my caregivers. The time before and after my surgery I fed my body and soul with positive messages and quality hugs. Some of those hugs I received from my daily talks with God, from my prayer sessions with good friends and my rabbi, from my family and especially my wonderful children and my beloved husband. I felt I had achieved my goal and was really so proud.

Avoid Comparisons

I remained committed to not invading my body and mind with war stories from well-meaning people. When a horror story slipped through the lips of others to my ears, I quickly reminded myself that I was an individual, with a unique body, my doctor was great, and that I would be fine.

Acknowledge Mistakes

There were times when I was feeling very sad about having to take this turn in the road in my life. I did cry, thus slipping into a state that went against my real beliefs. It was hard at times to keep practicing all my known health strategies. At those times, I did admit to defeat, and would have the support of family and friends to get back on the affirmative track. One anchor I utilized a few times was the remarks that Morrie made in *Tuesdays with Morrie*. He reflected how he gave himself permission to cry in the morning. The rest of the day he was not allowed to feel sorry for himself. Thank goodness my condition was nowhere near his level of seriousness but the technique was a good one to follow.

Stretch Out of a Comfort Zone

The process of getting ready for a serious operation, for staying in a hospital for several days, and for planning a six-week recovery period of which many included no steps or driving was a major stretch for me. I kept giving myself assignments to do each day that allowed me to prepare but not linger on the negative aspects. I even kept myself busy while waiting for the doctor to come and get me from the prep room. Alan and I were playing a "Name a Song Starting with a Specific Letter of the Alphabet" game. We had often played this while walking on the beach and it brought back happy memories while waiting for the unknown. In times past, just going to the dentist could make me have a stomach attack. The activities I did were truly a stretch but taught me a great lesson on my true capabilities.

Practice C+A=R

My result that I wanted was to have a most successful operation and recovery. In order to obtain that, I needed my actions to be such that I would maintain a positive attitude and follow my additional life-long beliefs. I was very cognizant of the responses I had to give to each circumstance in order to reach my desired result. I was absolutely, with the power and knowledge I had, committed to this formula. I stretched and stretched and I gratefully achieved my results!

Recognize My Successes

I felt so proud of each tiny step of my journey at this time. There were moments when I recognized the successes immediately. Often, I would found myself reflecting on what I had accomplished at other unique moments other than when they occurred. Usually, I shared these successes with loved ones. Frequently, I wrote them in my miracle journal. My esteem was high!

Becoming a Miracle Detective

I am fortunate that I regularly identify the many miracles that occur in my daily life. There is one particular miracle that I want to share. The day before surgery, while waiting for my hair to dry at the beauty shop, I reached for a magazine to read. The *Oprah* magazines are my favorites and I was lucky to find three. I decided to read the oldest edition as I was going to receive the latest copy from one of my daughters. It was at the very last page that Oprah shared her conversation with Maya Angelou. She commented how she was told by her mentor and friend that when you seem to have the most difficulties, or are feeling so low, that it was definitely time to stop and thank God for everything in your life. It ʳemed that the more you thanked him, the more bounty you ᵒgnized as having received.

ˡoved that thought. I had a plan as to when I could incorporate the ⁿto my life. The next day, as Alan and I were driving to the ˡ, I reflected on the article. I asked him to share aloud things he ful for and then I would do the same. A rule was that we could ᵒn an item once. I began by thanking God for inventing machines that could find my health problem and for individuals and instruments that could correct the situation.

I could have chosen any one of those three magazines. I believe it was a miracle that I chose that one. Because of the great feelings generated from this activity, I will facilitate it many times in the future with my family and friends.

Recreate a Treasured Memory

I immediately began collecting memorabilia that I wanted to take with me to create an inviting, environment during my stay in the hospital. Included among the items were my Miracles Happen banner, a favorite picture of my family and a very special red heart beaded bag, with rocks that had positive messages inside. These items made me reflect on the various ways I was lovable, capable, and special.

Perform an Act of Kindness

I really cannot think of one specific act of kindness that I performed at this time. One of my Granny Roses felt otherwise. She commented that my requesting something specific from my friends—omitting negative stories and questions from our conversations—enabled them to know what they could say or do for me at my difficult time. Someone else stated that I was unconditionally accepting and therefore made it easy for people to share their feelings for me. These are unusual acts of kindness that one rarely gives thought to except when a dear friend dialogues such opinions. Perhaps my greatest act of kindness will be in my positive role modeling to others as to the quality of life that can be obtained from healthy living strategies during difficult times.

Do Something Fun

One thing that I did was I shopped 'til I dropped as I was looking for bright, fancy nightgowns to wear in the hospital (as a sidenote, I had to wear the hospital gowns the entire stay due to the different tubes). It was fun! Another thing I did for fun was to have a manicure and a pedicure the day before surgery. And you won't believe this! I even bought a whistle for signaling the nurses. Someone once said that I might need one in case the nurses did not respond to my call within a reasonable amount of time. I would not have chosen to use it (my nurses were terrific) but when I looked at the whistle, it made me laugh.

One of my most memorable things that I did for fun was to make the time to meditate on a regular basis before and after the operation. I have always wanted to do this each day but time would slip away before I reached this goal. This activity brought me continual joy and peace. It also presented me with so many teachings about life.

One particular meditation was really special. I meditated right before leaving my house to go to the hospital. I received a message from this peaceful activity where I was told to share with others the importance of telling individuals how you cared about them. I even received a title for the message, "why wait?" The information obtained from that meditation filled my last moments at home with peace, reminded me that everything serves, served to reinforced my feelings that God continues to give me opportunities to take care of others, and helped strengthened my belief that I was truly one of God's special angels. I became so busy with writing about the message that I had received from this session that I was unaware the moment to leave for my operation had come.

Surround Yourself with Granny Roses

From reading my segment on Granny Rose, I know you can picture the type of person that would come under this category. How blessed I was to be able to search out as well as find so many of these individuals. I need to list my doctors first. They were wonderful, nurturing, and so very knowledgeable. I shared that they were now taking care of "Chicken Little." They all took great care of me!

My husband was incredible. After 36 year of marriage, all in good health, we were called upon to care for each other in a different way at this unique time. Alan created a loving, nurturing environment, answering any and all of my personal needs as defined by my professional team and myself. He was just outstanding!

Not to my surprise but to my wonderful delight, my children were terrifically supportive. They were by my side day and night offering physical and emotional support at every step of my journey to wellness. They became great nurses, cheerleaders, television critics, book reviewers and a great all-around entertainment crew.

My sister agreed to stay my first night with me. She knew my fears and was willing to do what she could to help elevate them. I will always be grateful for her love, especially at that time. Other family members were supportive in various ways as well and I was indeed grateful.

My friends were abundant and incredible. People from all walks of life whom I had touched in some positive way seemed to come forth and offer their love and support—from hugs and prayers and flowers and hugs and calls and hugs and candies and hugs and lunches and dinners and hugs. One of my buddies even left her family to serve as my nurse when I came up to my room from recovery. She was willing to forgo her plans so that I would feel that I was having extra-special care with no chance of mistakes. It is hard to adequately say thank you in words or actions for her inviting gesture. I am such a lucky, blessed individual.

And there were my rabbis, my special anchors in life. My senior rabbi was available for praying and listening and hugs always. My rabbi emeritus called from home to share prayers with me. These are two very special people in my life whom I have a very unique relationship with and know that I can call upon them anytime for their gifts of support, spiritual guidance, and love.

It is my hope and prayer, as we conclude our time together, that you will recognize ways to develop, maintain and increase the hugs in your life. As you practice living these strategies, I know that you will grow to recognize your self-worth and see yourself as being lovable, capable and special. I encourage you to reach out and help others to hug themselves. All of us together can create a more loving world for everyone.

Until we meet again…

Shalom, BB

"Each day provides its own gift."
Ruth Freedman

Printed in the United States
29801LVS00005B/430